Mighty Machines
FIRE TRUCKS
AND RESCUE VEHICLES

Jean Coppendale

QEB Publishing

A helicopter arrives to rescue people from a sinking boat.

If the sea is very rough and it is not safe for the lifeboats, helicopters are used to **hoist** people to safety.

Send an **ambulance!**

If someone has been badly **injured** or suddenly becomes very ill, an ambulance is called. The ambulance puts on its flashing lights and loud siren and rushes to help the person, or take the person to the hospital.

Inside the back of an ambulance is a bed, medical equipment, and somewhere for the **paramedics** to sit.

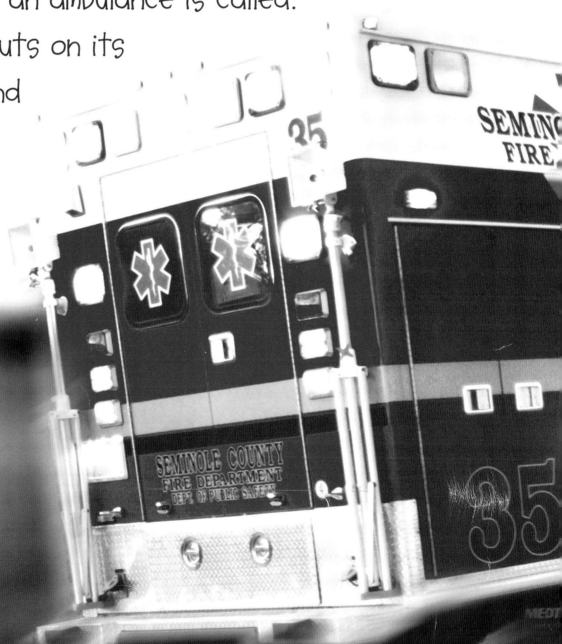

Some places are difficult to reach by road. An air ambulance helicopter is used instead.

Paramedics are people trained to care for the sick or injured person inside the ambulance.

Police on the way!

Police cars can race to the scene of a crime or accident. Police drivers have been trained to drive at high speeds on busy roads and highways.

Police cars have computers that allow officers to check information, such as if a car is stolen or not.

Sometimes a police helicopter is used to chase people on the roads who are speeding, or **criminals** who are trying to escape.

Motorcycle patrol

In very crowded cities, some police use motorcycles to help them reach an accident quickly or chase criminals through busy streets.

Sometimes motorcycle police travel with the cars of important people in order to keep them safe.

Motorcycle police always wear safety helmets and they have to be specially trained to ride their bikes.

Activities

- Start your own collection of emergency vehicle pictures. Group them together, for example ambulances, fire engines, police cars, and so on. Which are your favorites? Why?

- Do you know what each of these emergency vehicles is used for? What can you see in each picture?

- On a big sheet of paper, draw your favorite emergency vehicle. Then imagine there is a telephone call. There has been an accident. Quick, you must help! Make up a story about what happens next.

- Which vehicle does a police officer drive?

Glossary

Criminals
People who have broken the law by doing something such as stealing.

Goods
Things such as clothes, food, cars, or books. They can be moved by boat, plane, train, or truck.

Harbor
A safe place where ships and boats can stay. This is where boats unload and collect their goods and where passenger boats pick up and drop off people.

Hoist
To pull someone on board a plane or helicopter using a rope.

Injured
When someone has been hurt.

Paramedics
The men and women who drive the ambulance and care for injured people until they reach the hospital.

Passengers
People who travel inside a car, bus, train, boat, or airplane.

Pilots
The people who fly planes and helicopters.

Siren
A loud noise used by emergency vehicles when they are traveling very fast. It's used to warn other vehicles on the road that an emergency vehicle is coming through.

Vehicle
A car, truck, motorcycle, or anything else that travels on the road.

Index